DREAMCRAFT

THE HUGH MacLENNAN POETRY SERIES

Editors: Allan Hepburn and Carolyn Smart

Recent titles in the series

Dreamcraft

PETER DALE SCOTT

McGill-Queen's University Press
Montreal & Kingston • London • Chicago

ISBN 978-0-2280-2098-1 (paper)
ISBN 978-0-2280-2099-8 (ePDF)
ISBN 978-0-2280-2100-1 (ePUB)

Legal deposit second quarter 2024
Bibliothèque nationale du Québec

Printed in Canada on acid-free paper that is 100% ancient forest free
(100% post-consumer recycled), processed chlorine free

We acknowledge the support of the Canada Council for the Arts.

Nous remercions le Conseil des arts du Canada de son soutien.

McGill-Queen's University Press in Montreal is on land which long
served as a site of meeting and exchange amongst Indigenous Peoples,
including the Haudenosaunee and Anishinabeg nations. In Kingston
it is situated on the territory of the Haudenosaunee and Anishinaabek.
We acknowledge and thank the diverse Indigenous Peoples whose
footsteps have marked these territories on which peoples of the world
now gather.

Library and Archives Canada Cataloguing in Publication

Title: Dreamcraft / Peter Dale Scott.

Names: Scott, Peter Dale, author.

Series: Hugh MacLennan poetry series.

Description: Series statement: The Hugh MacLennan poetry series

Identifiers: Canadiana (print) 20230586783 | Canadiana
(ebook) 20230586791 | ISBN 9780228020981 (softcover) |
ISBN 9780228020998 (PDF) | ISBN 9780228021001 (ePUB)

Subjects: LCGFT: Poetry.

Classification: LCC PS8587.C637 D74 2024 | DDC C811/.54—dc23

This book was typeset by Marquis Interscript in 9.5/13 Sabon.

CONTENTS

Contents

DREAMCRAFT

PRESENCE

For Robert and Rebecca Tracy

i

In the corner of a field not ploughed
      where small trees were beginning to grow
    a well-worn horseshoe

In the flattened area
      next to the mossy grinding rock
    a pierced bone bead

and yes, in that chipping ground
      up behind Yosemite
    in the High Sierra

imperfect arrowheads
      amid the blaze
    of glinting obsidian flakes

We who feel inspired
      by the works of Hölderlin
    or the *Nimrod* of Elgar

the great enterprise to hunt down
      in art the ineffable
    should not forget that

at unexpected moments
        one can still feel and hear
     even in an abandoned field

what I can only call
        the presence
     albeit transitory

of something else

ii

Albeit transitory!
        the shoe nailed to the lintel
     of the old shed that by now

must have collapsed
        the bead strung on a necklace
     by a young woman

who lost it long before she died
        the arrowheads
     as I had given my word

left where they were

Just as cosmic space
       is knowable
   by those specks of light

at great distance from each other
       that we see again
   when not in cities

so the long stretch of life
       reveals its curvature
   by those widely separated

moments when we are
       brushed
   by this awareness

of an other
that we do not know

This is a universe
of moreness

Just as the cardinal flower
      has a throat that fits
  the length of the hummingbird bill

so an electron is precisely
      the interactions in its field
  and we who at first

care only for ourselves
      only become human
  from interactions with others

I think this is why Moshe
      taught us to love God   *Deuteronomy 6:5*
  with all of our heart

and all of our soul
      and all of our *meod*   מְאֹד
  which when I meditate

I am quite sure means
      what I sensed just now merging
  with the world around me

and which I can only describe
as moreness

I need to be clear about this
      Meod in dictionaries is defined   מְאֹד
   as *force* or *muchness* or *abundance*

But what I mean
      is not that force of id
   which troubled me for decades

as a Buddhist I used to think
      escape from that self
   was into non-being

but now I am content to pass
      into the space of moreness
   that way less than electric field

where I stood beside Maylie
      cooking in the bunkhouse
   after picking apricots all day

and where I first saw
      my four-pound daughter Cassie
   cupped in a nurse's hand

and where I shared with a friend
      a low smoky sunrise
   from a mountain top in Tennessee

what I still feel when Ronna
      asleep in bed
   stirs when I think of rising

and drapes her arm across me

           iii

Our need as humans –
to be more than we are

People have to get it
the universe is not as Newton

is said to have imagined
a timeless clockwork

it has a history
and like ourselves

and our thin sliver of ethogeny   *cultural evolution*
is getting somewhere

A Poem for Election Day, 8 November 2022

Earth! You seem so solid
        when I plant my feet squarely
    to pick up the newspaper

but this morning when there is sun
        I am reminded
    that it rises now

not over the Boder-Billings' driveway
        but two houses further south
    in Susan Blew's redwoods

a wobble saving us
        from eternal rainless summer
    These deep movements

that affect us most
        are ones we cannot discern
    the erratic wobble through time

of rising and collapsing empires
        behind which a still deeper shift
    appears not to be cyclical –

the entropic spread
        of the drifting cosmos
    after the big bang

or the violent disruptions
        of decaying cultures
    making space for new ones

like the end of the Bronze Age
        the collapse of Babylon and Mycenae
    with those quarreling rapist gods

remembered in Homer
        along with Linear B
    restricted to palace sites

clearing a permanent space
        for the spread of monotheism
    and demotic alphabets

as with the collapse of Rome
        a further clearing
    when the torrent of invading Vandals

after sacking Mainz and Trier
        put a final end
    to that practice (which could only

have been developed and refined
        in a slave-owning city)
    of watching for entertainment

gladiators be killed

The OED defines
both mythopoeia and mythogenesis
as the same: *the creation of myths*

This is to tell the OED
the two are not the same
but different aspects of creation

For mythopoeia think Tolkien
or even Salome
who according to Matthew
danced at Herod's court
instructed by her mother
and was rewarded with what she asked for
John the Baptist's head   *Matthew* 14:8

From this Wilde's drama
had Salome kiss the head
Huysmans described her
as *the Beast of the Apocalypse*
and Strauss added
from another source
the Dance of the Seven Veils

this was conscious myth-making
which we expect from art
in a secular era

but in mythogenesis
the mind does not make something up
something occurs to it
or maybe just happens in it
in response perhaps
to the purposive needs of DNA

as in the case
of my artless
former student

who told me her most memorable
moment at university
had been when I was lecturing
on Dante's *Paradiso*
and a white dove
flew into the classroom

remembering the event
I replied to her
it was not the *Paradiso*
and I was certain the bird had been
a brown California towhee

undaunted she replied
in total confidence
Oh no Professor Scott
it was a white dove

like peasants recalling
the miracles of St Martin
for Sulpicius Severus
may this help us
be more understanding of
if not sympathetic to

the dawn of a Dark Age

Harry harry the winds home
over Turkeycock Hill

where the cows in their well-worn tracks
trail homewards and disappear

our hundred-year-old empty unsafe barn
once creaking and swaying

is now as still

as the squat
square-timbered icehouse

the sleepy creek
under its dense bushes

the sand dunes where my mother found
a Louis Seize penny

this evening star

it is time

to leave the grown-ups downstairs
around the mantled kerosene lamp

and be alone
with the bedside candle
flickering

and the whippoorwill

SHIVA CANDLE

In memory of Daniel Ellsberg, d. 16 June 2023

This morning as I meditate
        in touch with my vital breath
    I see Dan's candle

with a flickering flame
        converting just like me
    its carbons into CO_2

beside the memorial rose
        which in exact contrast
    is sucking up water

to exhale pure oxygen
        mysterious complementarity
without which we would not survive

Now Dan's breathing has stopped
        but not his presence
    which helped refresh our culture

in mysterious complementarity –
        like a forest refreshing nature
or Wilberforce a slaving Britain –

at first to the Vietnam war
        which by then even Wall Street
    was saying cost too much

and then as a model
      for whistleblowing in general
   a word which in 1971

the year of the Pentagon Papers
      was added by the OED   *Oxford English*
   to the English language   *Dictionary*

followed in 1989
      by the Whistleblower Protection Act
   a significant baby step

towards our distant goal
      of an open society
   which someday might help restrain

a global military system
      already showing signs
   that its time will soon run out   *Hudson in Blinova*

like this flickering candle
      in a world Dan then helped change
   as he began to practice

fifty years of nonviolent
      satyagraha   truth action
   fasting for thirteen days

on the steps of the Pentagon
      to protest the war in Nicaragua   *Liteky*
   in what is thought of

as *civil disobedience*
  when in fact it is rather
 obedience

to the highest authority we know
that truth we carry within us

BOB SILVERS AND THE DEEP STATE

In Memoriam: Robert B. Silvers
31 December 1929–20 March 2017

The gentlest genius I ever met
      was you Bob
  who enlarged our *Overton window*

those *few ideas or scenarios*
      the public is willing to consider   *Levingston*
  sometimes using the art of *ketman*   *Milosz*
                              Captive Mind 57–8
the *science of dissimulation*   *Hitchens*
      in the service of truth
  that Milosz used in post-war Poland   *Milosz Native*
                                  Realm 269
Still vivid though forty years ago
      those lunches at Patsy's
  our walk on the fire trail high above Berkeley

as the sun was setting in the Golden Gate
      the trail dust gathering
  on your immaculate Ferragamo shoes

these stellar events in my life
      were not just memorable
  they were spiritual

You edited so many books
      but you never wrote one
  preferring to guard and expand

in the *New York Review of Books*
    what could be discussed in higher circles
  in that crazy era when

the anger of the antiwar movement
    helped elect Richard Nixon   *in 1968*
  all of us were a little touched

and you Bob had to live down
    your front page of a Molotov cocktail   *Kimball*
  and Kopkind's *morality like politics*   *ibid.*

starts at the barrel of a gun   *Kopkind 90*
    But as novelists and poets
  took on the *system*

attempting with Allen Ginsberg
    to levitate the Pentagon
  you however fallibly

took on our *épistème*   *Foucault 54*
    examining its limits   *Kermode*
  towards the *Unspeakable*   *Merton*

that darkness where in those days
    the *Spirit of History*   *Milosz "Treatise*
  howled like Cerberus in its cave *on Poetry" 128*

On the Vietnam and Iraq wars
    you *presented viewpoints*
  hard to get in established media   *Sherman 5*

as when you published Ellsberg
        on the Laotian air war   *Ellsberg*
    before he had leaked the Papers   *Pentagon Papers*

or when you let me ask
        of the alleged *intercept* –   *Scott "Tonkin Bay"*
    (*the "smoking gun" evidence needed* –

according to LBJ –
        to justify air strikes)   *Hanyok 24,*
    showing that the second attack   *Johnson 114–15*

on US destroyers in the Tonkin Gulf
        did in fact take place
    (when we're now positive it didn't)

could it *deliberately*
        have been fed in
    by American intelligence personnel?   *Scott*
                               "Tonkin Bay"

We wrestled with that question
        for perhaps an hour
    and got an OK from Bill Bader

Fulbright's expert on Tonkin Gulf   *Proctor*
        with *a background in naval intelligence* *Woods 475*
    (*but really* – you said – *CIA*)   *cf. Tracy n67*

who had all the right clearances
        yet at the Senate Committee Hearing
    with the future of the War at stake

was not allowed to remain in the room   Scott *The War*
      I see now how your mediating   *Conspiracy 139*
  between the Mandate of History

and my own naïve anti-war concerns
      then and also after   Scott *"Old Wealth"*
  the CIA had impounded

an essay I innocently thought
      I could mail to *Ramparts*   *ibid.*
  when you now let Bill Bader veto

my essay about the *Pueblo*   Scott The *War Conspiracy*
      was as to others *more loyal to me*   *178–215*
    than I was to myself   *Lilla*

Your most ambitious attempt
      to expand the *Overton window*   *Levingston*
  was to publish *The Second Oswald*   *Popkin*

after which you changed my life
      by introducing me to Popkin
  and through him the Committee

to Investigate Assassinations
      You continued to publish
  into your eighties

useful fragments preparing
      our post-imperium
  for a prevailable future

from Judt on the Holocaust   *Judt*
        to visionary essays
    on the early Christian church   *Finley*

And you called back once again
        to suggest I should write with Gore Vidal
    about Kennedy's murder

until Gore's four phone calls to me
        were all (as I could have predicted)
    broken off in mid-sentence

followed by the operator's
        false claim to you that my phone
    was *not currently in service*   *Scott Coming*
                                              to Jakarta 134
Just as phone breaks in mid-broadcast
        terminated my longtime practice
    of talks on Pacifica radio   *KPFA KPFK*

you and Gore then backed off
        accepting this clear warning
    from a deadlier level of the meta-system

than that realm of mere words
        you shared with the Agency   *CIA*
    leaving me heartbroken –

in the midst of my other losses   *Scott Poetry and*
        not one but two friends murdered   *Terror 23 199*
    my father's mind gone astray –   *Djwa 451*

that we would not be working together
        But now   as I reflect
   on how Gary Webb was destroyed

by both the *Times* and the *Post*
        before he shot himself   *Grim*
   as did my friend Mike Ruppert

after his offices were trashed
        and he failed to restart his life –   *Stroud*
   I am not sorry but grateful

you taught me the virtue of discretion
        which may explain my survival
   And I ignore the claim

from a hostile right-wing critic
        that you once were *army intelligence*   *Kimball*
   the fact that those first two reviews

you ever worked for
        were both creations of the CIA   *Whitney 1–16*
   these do not now concern me

I want only to thank you
        for enlarging our épistème
   in your way very gently

toward greater freedom
and greater kindness

                5 April 2017–10 April 2018

WHAT I SEE WHEN I GO OUT
TO PICK UP THE PAPER DURING COVID

For Galia and Peter Szurley

> *(when you turn ninety-two*
> *the less you get to travel*
> *the more you get to see)*

the sunlight through redwood branches
across the street
hitting the Szurleys' orange tree
behind our purple princess bush
and their neat bronze hedgerow
of trembling beeches out to the sidewalk

and beyond them a pink tulip treetop
and the white star magnolia
against a clean blue sky
the tower of the old School for the Blind
nestling in its trees
like that church in Auvergne I could not get to

and as I pick up the *Times*
its black headlines seen through a blue wrap
the wet stains on the concrete
the grass next to it sparkling
from last night's rain

7 January 2021

Turning back toward home
        on my after-breakfast walk
    I face the steep bluff of eucalyptus

that stands over our neighbourhood
        and am struck by the beauty
    of what can hardly be seen

for today after heavy rain
        the highest levels are obscured
    like the truth of the Tao Te Ching

by the low-lying duvet of cloud
        the farthest trees barely visible
    looking remote as if ranged

on some twelfth-century Chinese scroll
        Tell me! What is it in our
    bicameral brain that makes

obfuscation of mere fact
so much more beautiful?

MINDING: TO CHELSEA MANNING

Cf. Paul Daley, "'All lies': How the US Military Covered Up Gunning Down Two Journalists in Iraq," Guardian, 14 June 2020, https://www.theguardian.com/us-news/2020/jun/15/all-lies-how-the-us-military-covered-up-gunning-down-two-journalists-in-iraq.

You watched the pilots
of a US drone and chopper –
using language more suited
for a video game
nice missile   sweet   Ha Ha! –
shoot first a Reuters team
whose camera they thought was a gun
and then the arriving medics

not well fitted
for the military
you *minded* what you'd seen
and knowing that society
might take a long time
to forgive you
you went public with it

thereby changing
your youthful career
from intelligence analyst
to prisoner in solitary
with an initial sentence
of thirty-five years –

and already changing also
in a small significant way
the *enmindment* of the world
in which we can glimpse
our true history
slowly unfolding

TO DR CHRISTINE BLASEY FORD

i

At fifteen you endured
        a push from behind
    onto a bed

a drunken attempt
        to rip your clothes off
    hand over your mouth and nose

uproarious laughter

ii

Later you forced
        a US Justice – under oath –
    to evade obvious questions

a reluctant president
        to put up a charade
    of a pseudo-investigation

and men as well as women
        across the continent
    to reconsider the violence

in their own lives

History is very slow
      and yet I believe
   with Milton in *Areopagitica*

in the long run
      yours is the force
   that will prevail

sometimes
      as in the Dred Scott case
   you have to lose

      in order to win

DREAMING MY DNA

In an hour of sleep
        not fully sleep
    two very abstract rhyming dreams

the first of repotting
        the second a recurring dream
    about a chapter in my Milosz book

on revising another chapter
        Two dreams not reprising
    my *Tagesreste*

but maybe my DNA's –
        that I myself am a repotting
    of my DNA

already repotted
        in each of my grandchildren
    which – if Lamarck is right

in his conjecture
        that DNA is memory
    carrying with it the scars

not just of my recent COVID
        but also of the Black Death
    my DNA itself was dreaming

just as the complex DNA
        of Mary Shelley   nineteen
    compounding that of her father   *William Godwin*

and *its reasoning powers*
        with that of her mother   *Mary Wollstonecraft*
    under the empire of feeling

and also *the loss of a mother*
        dreamt about birthing a *monster*   *Vital Artifice*
    And what if each molecule

of my dreaming DNA
        was healthy not deformed
    like an acorn

carrying within it
        beyond anything
    we can conceive

the very concrete image
        of a shining oak tree
    each one of us

a shining leaf

Look! There between
      the half-hidden liquidambar
   at the corner of our house

and the redwood beyond it
      is the almost-full moon
   white and frail as a shred of Kleenex

I focus my mind on it
      until slowly I can begin
   to see it rising

or rather to watch myself
      beginning to descend
   in the quiet rush to the east

of everything around me
      this small green courtyard
   the trees of our neighbourhood

at my back the street corner
      where this morning two dogs
   snarled briefly at each other

and still further back where the sun
      will soon be hidden
   as the Golden Gate rises

my heart empties
          and very slowly
     the moon appears

to climb a bit faster
          and then even faster
     wobbling a little

like an errant balloon
already clear of the trees

THE IMPORTANCE OF A GARDEN

In Memoriam Judith Stronach

The poet Zbigniew Herbert once wrote
There are those who grow gardens in their heads
Contrasting himself with the great romantics
Such as in our time Judith Stronach
Judith wished dangerously to make the world
A little kinder
She summered on a small Bosnian island
Trying to mother orphans from that war
And week after week she tried to teach poetry
To the disadvantaged in West Oakland
Her frustrations bringing her more and more to accept
The importance of a garden
Just as her life was also a maze
And she designed on this hillside a maze
In the Old World style   a pattern
For reenacting our bafflement and loss
So in the same spirit she invented a garden
Where she could not stop the cat from catching lizards
But managed to give us on the West Coast
A *hortus conclusus* out of Tuscany
With hedges trimmed to an architectural plan
In keeping with that single noble row
Of Lombardy cypresses
Wholly at odds with the chaparral around them
High up above us on the hill
That help us, as we drive up Claremont Avenue

To remember her generous life
Of great beauty
In great pain.

DREAMCRAFT

For Leonard Cohen, d. 7 November 2016

[I   Before the Dream]

Lipizzaner – after my embarrassment
　　　　coming away on the bus
　　from yesterday's funeral

and talking to a woman
　　　　whom I knew very well
　　but could not *remember her name*

at least I recovered this word
　　　　by recalling the sand and sawdust
　　of the Winterreitschule

at the far end of the Hofburg　　　　　　*imperial palace*
　　　　where for eight weeks I worked
　　at a United Nations Conference

and where my Canadian amendment
　　　　by a large majority
　　defeated that of the French

in the tall Hall of Mirrors
　　　　one of which I rightly suspected
　　was a secret door

through which one Sunday
	I sneaked into a twisting hall
	past abandoned rooms

until I reached the imperial
	loge in the Hofkapelle *court chapel*
	where I looked down at

the Viennese Boys Choir
	singing a Mozart Mass –
	a layer of memories

from an overly-structured life
	I soon quit as too meaningless
	and returned to the battleground

of my painful college years
	from which last night's dream –

[II   The Dream]

   the *ruby* in its antique setting

to be *crushed* by me and Faye
	in a *handled loving-cup*
	which would yield a *draught of grand passion*

and access to *the Cave of Buried Winds*   *cf. Aeneid 1:52*
	but Faye and I never crushed it
	only *sipped* from that *cup of crushed ice*

as from *a piña colada*
>> Faye then devastated
> by the death of *her sister* whose *name*

kept escaping me in the dream
>> a championship swimmer drowned
> when her canoe tipped over

sparing her fiancé   *Peter Burgess*
>> just out from months in hospital
> who thirty years later as he stood

alone in a Berkeley party corner
> I was able to recognize and *name*

[III   Waking from the Dream]

As I slowly woke

why did I so obsess
>> about yesterday's failure on the bus
> to recover Barbara's *name*

besides not crushing that *ruby*
>> to gain access to the *Cave*
> in which I relived

my years-long anxiety
>> that I lacked *the daring*   *Dostoyevsky, cf. Lowe*
> to be a poet

which would explain my need
      after our house burned
    to start teaching right away   *Scott*

choosing *liberation from anxiety*
      rather than to confront it   *Heidegger*
   as if my fear of *passion*

had meant I had lost the chance
      to be enlightened   *cf. Ferrone*
  (*love more discerning*

as Mickiewicz wrote
      than lenses or learning)   *Mickiewicz*
  and even called into question

my career preaching nonviolence
      secure in my ivory turret?
  In short I again felt inferior

as if I had somehow failed
      to be ruthless enough
  to crush that *ruby* –

the way Goethe (as I'd read)
      dreamt of entering a walled garden
  with perfect assurance

and then passing through a door
      took by the ears
  a girl who had just punched him

and kissed her repeatedly   *Goethe*
      the way you Leonard in your teens
   hypnotized the family maid

till you got her to undress
      the way Roosevelt to ensure
   the success of D-Day

overruling Churchill's good concerns
      about *eighty thousand French casualties*   *Jordan*
   ordered the destruction

of the French railroad system
      the way in the *crise d'octobre*   *Quebec 1970*
   my father encouraged Pierre Trudeau

to invoke the War Measures Act   *Marshall, May*
      which preserved the rule of law
   by suspending it   and sent

five hundred people to jail
      among them two poets
   and my mother's good friend

the singer Pauline Julien –
      all this I feared like Milosz
   was Darwin's law of evolution

the triumph of the strong   *Milosz "Treatise on Theology,"*
      but at last I see it only   *cf. The Witness of Poetry*
   as one moment towards

that unresolved question
        who *shall inherit the earth*?

[IV   Postscript]

Leonard it was only when you died

for the first time I realized
        I was so freaked by forgetting Barbara's *name*
        because we were leaving the funeral

of Carl a loving father
        who had died too young from MS
        to ever be remembered as a poet

and this had made me remember
        my own years of unfulfillment
        in the shadow of my father's

poetic eminence in Montreal
        where he seduced many women
        (sending – I've since learned –

one husband to an asylum)   *Graham*
        unlike my mother who accepted
        for the sake of both their callings

the renunciation of a great love   *Clarkson*
        with Beth the future hero   *Norman Bethune*
        of the Chinese revolution

whose tomb is now a national shrine
    and above all your shadow Leonard
  you were five years my junior yet already

envied by me for being
    a lady's man with a car
  while completing your first book of poems

already larger than life
    as you still were that last June
  so afflicted you could barely move

when we played "You Want It Darker"
    great art even though I disagree
  which is why millions of people

from here to Kraków
    including myself
  still love you and are grateful

though just as I could not parse
    the two other women in the dream
  I could make no sense of then

Faye's sister whose *name*
    I now recall was *Barbara*   *Barbara Rodriguez*
  (*yes! like the Barbara on the bus*)

and *Eva* who dined alone   *Eva Dollfuss*
    at the table next to us
  still crushed by the weight of her father's –

the Austrian Bundeskanzler's – murder
        by a band of marauding Nazis
    inside – as I have just learned

by researching my dream –
        the Hofburg (*the Lipizzaner!*)   *Sachar*
    so also with you now gone

I have lost that urge to regret
        my own more tempered life
    of missed opportunities

from *the desire not to inflict pain* –
        which as Eliot admitted
    can be *near to cowardice*   *Gordon*

and was his excuse for disappointing
        his lover who had waited so long
    as well as mine with Faye

still vulnerable from her sister's death
        and my leaving so soon for Paris
    and as well as with Jane at the lake

Yaffa under the Chardin
        Ghislaine the French viscountess
    in the Tyrolean chalet

her face still fresh from skiing
        always preserving myself
    for *something precious*

a life which led me to Milosz
>   the *Gorgias* northern Thailand
>   never forgetting

that unforgettable jolt
>   of benign electricity
>   the first time when Faye

sitting to my left
>   in her white angora sweater
>   turned to smile at me

and by chance we touched

BECOMING

The first reaching out
of a pear tree —

even more so
when cultivated

than the wild blighted original —
is its blossom

white petals spread open
against the clear sky blue

to show black dots of pollen
on whiskery stamens I can barely see

ready to be probed and ravaged
by greedy insects

before the petals fall on us
replaced by leaves

inhaling the dirty city air
to breathe out oxygen

And we   past all breeding
when we open out our minds

like an Anjou pear
are not fully developed

until enjoyed –

What comfort   not just when it's bright
        and the yellow sorrels
     open their crowded faces

but when it's cloudy or cold
        and their closed heads droop
     in dejection

Scientists call this *nyctinasty* –
        a light-induced *nastic*
     or *non-directional*   response –

controlled by the amount
        potassium ions are moved
     between surrounding tissue

and the stalk's *pulvinus* –
        an enlarged section at the stem's base
     subject to changes of turgor

* * *

Though eighteenth-century empiricists
        doubted *insensate matter*
     could give rise to sensory experience

it is now standard in physics
        to say *an electron feels*
     its *microscopic high-frequency field*

and when I snuggle into bed
        next to Ronna sleeping
     in our own small energy field

I feel enlightened
        as my heart's turgor
     expands deeper into oneness

with you   dearest Ronna
and you   bright sorrels of the earth

For Ronna

A red rose
in a crystal shot glass
on a white kitchen tablecloth

After the tsunami
when you walked down the line of bloated corpses
with the parents who'd flown in from New York

to identify the newlywed
by her engagement ring
you planted a rose garden

I'm not talking now
about all those memories
only the clear voice

at this moment
inside me
whispering

This!

The hysterical howls of the Beat poets are the rebellion
of a well-brought-up muse, a return to their native tradition
[i.e., Whitman], somewhat vulgar but still authentic.

Czeslaw Milosz

i

Flight (Uczieczka)

Czeslaw   in your eight-line poem
        you and Janka
    were fleeing the burning city   NCP 74

with what you could carry on your back
        until on the road
    in a time of general starvation

you were robbed even of that
        now totally liberated
    from your entitled past

you had to dig
        potatoes for a week
    just so you could reach

that country manor outside Kraków
        right before it was looted
    by the Soviet armies

in a barbarism you compared
        to the sack of Rome by the Goths
   the world was all before you

you closed your eight-line poem
       we are fated to beget
   a new and violent tribe

and the earth was opened
       by a sword of flames   *ibid.*
   much later you added

that from the death
       of the Republic
Comes man, naked and mortal

Ready for truth, for speech, for wings   *A Treatise*
                                         on Poetry 54

ii

Treatise on Poetry (Traktat poetycki)

From western Europe
       in the grip of its demonic forces   *ibid. 113*
   you wrote *I would like to be*

a poet of the five senses
       That's why I don't become one   NCP 170
   the *eternal moment*

did not attract you *as it should*   *A Treatise on Poetry 58*
     you wanted instead
   to raise *the dust of events*   *ibid.*

but after you left
     for America   *and its eternal*
  rotation of seasons   *ibid. 113*

no longer in the shadow
     of a nationalist church
  and *that crazy St Dominic*   *Merton and Milosz 133*

but where *the oaks*
     perfect the shadow of May leaves   *NCP 184*
  you wrote to the Trappist Thomas Merton

In spite of all my hatred for the Thomists
     I know that the only subject for a poet
   is the verb "to be"   *Merton and Milosz 133*

and in verse   *Only this*
     is worthy of praise
   Only this:

the day   *NCP 184*

Throughout Our Lands (Po ziemi naszej)

Czeslaw we met in Berkeley
    when it was still newly aroused
  by a brief and gentle revolution

when for a very short while
    before they mass-marketed
  The Summer of Love

women walked braless in see-through blouses
    and your id acknowledged
  that beneath the sprinklered lawns

where the girls *came back from the tennis courts*
    devils *were turning somersaults*   *ibid.*
  which you later confessed   *ibid. 611*

were the *diabolic dwarfs* in yourself   *ibid.*
    Like the shipwrecked Cabeza de Vaca *c. 1488–1560*
  among Gulf Coast tribes   *"Álvar Núñez*
             Cabeza de Vaca"

on a *seven years march to California*   *NCP 187*
    you soon *adapted*
  to the lives of the indigenous

not able thereafter
          to be a true European
     you for a very short while

dispensed with pessimism
          wrote – in our translation –
     give them a few stones

and edible roots, and they will build the world
          adding   *On all fours!*
     Who has not dreamt of naked nuns?

Smear our thighs with war paint
Lick the ground. Wha ha, hu hu.   *ibid. 186–8*

                         iv

               To jest i tylko to jest ocalenie

1964
          when our poem was published   *Encounter*
     your first poem ever to appear in English   *February 1964*

(*translated* you wrote
          by Peter Dale Scott
     with my minor assistance)   *Postwar Polish*
                                                   Poetry vii
was the year of the F S M   *Free Speech Movement*
     and the passionate faculty assembly
     to support the students' demands

(which you later dismissed as *Maoist madness*   ABCS 230
            although Mario Savio   FSM *leader*
    who had been beaten in Mississippi

was fighting for Freedom Summer)   *Cohen 59–60*
            that solemn assembly in which
    we voted on opposite sides

Was this the key
            to the end of our happy years
    of drunken collaboration

or was it that meeting
            to oppose the Vietnam war
    where you had seen me on the panel

with Chomsky whom you called
            in a tone foreboding
    my imminent expulsion

one of those intellectuals
            who destroyed Weimar
    a charge which I disputed

or was it your Warsaw poem
            with its good question
    What is poetry that does not save

nations or peoples   *NCP 77*
            that I fought to *translate*
    That I wanted good poetry

without knowing it   *ibid.*
      (like a lover able to see
    he is *only one among many*

who thus heals his heart *without knowing it*)   *ibid. 50*
    this is and only this is salvation
    while you no longer a bard

in your communal culture
    but now just a poet
    in this new and softer *episteme*

insisted on blurring that line
    to make it personal
    In this and only this

I find salvation?   *ibid. 77*

v

Orpheus and Eurydice

When Janka died in Berkeley   *Milosz's first wife*
    you wrote an American poem
    recalling your life together

campfires, fires of burning cities   NCP 469
    you confessed *I betrayed her with women,*
    though faithful to her only.   *ibid.*

But now back in the Poland
        you helped to liberate –
    forgetful of when in Paris

you considered your poetry
        a kind of higher politics   Native Realm 247
    those words you'd written *for your drawer*   *secretly*

You who wronged a simple man
        Do not feel safe. The poet remembers   NCP 103
    now in steel on the Gdańsk memorial –

you now ninety   the survivor
        of so many matrices of thought
    from Russia to America

channelled the bard doomed   *Orpheus*
        to be torn apart by Maenads
    standing on the flagstones

of the sidewalk
        at the entrance of Hades
    and responding to Carol's death   *Milosz's second*
                                                          wife
with a nine-stringed lyre
        he yielded to the dictation of a song
    And so Hermes brought forth Eurydice

A steep climbing path phosphorized
        But under his faith a doubt sprang up
    he turned his head

and behind him on the path
      was no one
   And he fell asleep with his cheek

on the sun-warmed earth   *Second Space 99–102*
      and soon you too were gone
   but still with us

behind you on the path

                              17 January 2021

THE FOREST OF WISHING

The hu-hu-hu of tribes, hot bramble of the continent.
But afterward?

Czeslaw Milosz

Here Eden has no more walls
no more angels to herd you in
it is endless.

Sunshine, and wind
the sea's surf just visible
and almost noiseless

and even lifting the hem of pain
within you, just as along as
your eyes can focus

The rest is loss

beautiful, endless
nothing in this forest punishes
the jungle opens to your every wish.

Wherever you want to, you can get to.
Look, a mermaid on a rock!
You are Neptune with trident

scudding toward her in the play of foam
curled in a darling aureole
the waters slewing under your naughty lilo

or, if you like to see yourself writ large
you can launch into the air
a millionaire.

Why why not?
macaw cobra ocelot
the amulet of your radiant heart
tells you you need not fear them

friends in the jungle
long alligator striped piranha
the dangerous things you have seen in solaria
prissy hummingbird torpid python.

Not Caesar any more or Vergil
or Cecil B. de Mille
(can you tell from this a wish is like crying
and as anonymous?)

you stare back at the abandoned gear
of your resolves
wondering how you in that caravanserai
ever moved so slowly

how it was the four walls of the day
earth water fire air
did not before this transport fall away.

Now, if you are in love with God, allay
this green reality of wishes
with the confusion
of resolution

as amid jungle shouts of wishing
your feet tread up water, joy on joy,
you can still recognize those feet,
and hate them.

Papaya? Ondine? Breadfruit?
As much as childhood, this word "crave" bores you.

Forest, scream.
Troops, advance.
Now wilt, self-consciousness, or hate yourself!

THAT MOMENT

I still do not understand
what that moment was

an ordinary moment
when picking the *Times*

from the wet concrete driveway
under the blue sky

trees back in their autumn color
my eyes close to the leaves

that carpeted the lawn
catching flecks of sunlight

an ordinary moment
and exactly then

a glimpse of something
I could not see

TO MY DAUGHTER IN WINNIPEG

In April, after the star magnolias
and tulip trees
have finished showing off

the hesitant maples
like shy Canadians
almost as an afterthought

push out their tiny pink
spinners

LEONARD AND PETER

For Leonard Cohen (1934–2016)
(Cf. Leonard Cohen, The Flame, 159–60)

Leonard
(from his DVD, *21 September 2016):*

You want it darker / We kill the flame ...

Peter *(casual inscription in his book,*
Walking on Darkness,
1 October 2016):

If *you* want it darker
This book is not for you
I have always wanted it lighter
And I think God does too

Leonard *(email, 3 October 2016):*

who says "i" want it darker?
who says the "you" is "me"?
god saved you in your harbour
while millions died at sea

you and god are buddies
you know his wishes now
here's broken Job all bloodied
who met him brow to brow

there is a voice so powerful
so easily unheard
those that hear may hate it all
but follow every word

if you have not been asked
to squat above the dead
be happy that you're deaf
not something worse instead

he will make it darker
he will make it light
according to his torah
which leonard did not write

Peter (email, 4 October 2016):

Who says I know God's wishes?
I've not met brow to brow
never had a chance to glimpse him
and never hope to now

But we who were raised in harbours
while others burned from war
have been free to choose which voices
made us what we are.

66

Leonard (email, 4 October 2016):

That was great fun.
Be well, dear friends.
Much love,
Eliezer

Leonard (text, 6 November 2016,
in response to photo of Peter with Sophia,
daughter of Rebecca de Mornay):

Blessed are the peacemakers: for they shall be called the
children of God.

FOR LEONARD COHEN (1934–2016)

i
YouTube 11 November

Their woolen collars turned up
they shuffle in front of the unused brick doorway
heaped up with futureless flowers

in a chill Montreal
November greyness
still under your spell

who have hypnotized them
though you are gone now
no one is speaking

except for one or two
in front of other cameras

ii
Recalling November 1955

This silence speaks for me
How can one make poetry
out of numbness?

Or capture that magic I first felt
along with our difference
when you an undergraduate

drove me a first-year professor
who did not know how to drive
to see our girlfriends in Massachusetts?

As light slowly turned to dark
in the deep valleys of Vermont
with their covered bridges

we discussed for miles and miles
the horrors of World War Two
I already drawn to question

you to grasp
I to investigate the world
you to experience it

and become a bard

iii

Congregation Beth Israel, Berkeley, 26 November

My sense of opportunity and failure
after my efforts in Shul

to describe your *presence*
left me feeling both worthless

and also naked and alert
as after my father's and mother's deaths

when I also had to speak while feeling numb
very late last night

in bed in an almost
fetal position

my head between the blades
of my dear wife's back

I heard this infant inside me
howling for no reason

and then a calming voice
time a relentless river

in which millions of good people
are being swept away

and where the only
safe direction to venture out

is upstream

iv
Memorial Service, Los Angeles, 11 December

And now in LA the choir
from Shaar Hashomayim in Montreal
sings from the opening of Kaddish

magnified sanctified
and *hineini hineini Here I am*
just as they did

in your final album
I think *How outrageous*

that they dare sing the chorus
to *You Want It Darker*

without your low
dominating voice

I'm out of the game
it is only later

that I hear this violation
as deliberate *negative sound*

defining your absence

v

at the time when I heard
the word *hineini Here I am*
I wanted to feel it was still true

but your rabbi recalling
your deep interest in *kabbalah*
said the one thing you did not believe

was the immortality of the soul
So in your gesture of saying
I am ready my Lord

was that just something to entertain
us people huddled in a lifeboat
before it too founders?

Or unlike those
who were mere entertainers
did you intend to resurrect

the importance since Job
of quarreling with God?

vi

and now at the door it's time
to kiss for a final good-bye

Charley the Webb sister
who on stage with Leonard

would turn a cartwheel

7 November–11 December 2016

COMMISSAR AND YOGI

For Leonard Cohen (1934–2016)

*Tyrannical and despotic governments actually lack power
according to Arendt, because power occurs between people
who speak and act together in concert and does not concern
the sheer brute force necessary to make one's will appear
in the world.*

Karin Fry, *Arendt*

Two kinds of power
domination by force

versus the human power
of persuasion

In Warsaw I was a consul
assigned to deny visas

to young women I judged
might be marriageable

and when I had to tell
the more beautiful ones

smiling in front of me
with flowers in their hair

they would have to apply
through Ottawa

for a permanent visa
they would go down on their knees

burst into tears and beg
which after a while

I began to dream about
erotically

till I arranged to quit

while at the Isle of Wight
rock festival ten years later

when the angry thousands
set fire to the equipment

Jimi Hendrix could not handle them
so they woke you Leonard and brought you out

to calm them by singing
like a bird on a wire

and Joan Baez said later
only Leonard could have done it

his poetry   magic
I pray for a world

when the only power there will be
is that power you Leonard

still have
even in death

to make strangers cry

EPITHALAMIUM

For Norma Kaufman and Henry Hirschel

*The most beautiful flowers sometimes bloom on the edge
of the abyss.*

Czeslaw Milosz

· At a time when
      as so often the world
   is once again parched –

forests nearby are burning
      the seas have toxic tides
   even the air is threatened

and the stricken creeks choked
      with ash cry out again
   your cities are burned with fire –   Isaiah 1:7

under this green canopy
      of Californian live oaks
   and Berkeley tree-ferns

is a unique *huppah* –
      from clothes of a deceased husband
   with jewels from a deceased wife –

sewn by Norma a widow whose life
      was sown in tears
   but who today – the day after

Shabbat Nachamu
      the first Shabbat of Consolation
and *Tisha b'Av*

The Shabbat
of Comfort

the destruction of the temple
      Comfort, comfort my people,
  her hard service has been completed –

Nachamu
nachamu ami
Isaiah 40:1–2

marries Henry a widower –
      whose father when just fifteen
was sent off alone from Hamburg

to escape via Vladivostok
      then wedded here in America
a survivor from Dresden –

and now Norma and Henry together
      break yet again a glass
which last time for them symbolized

the finality of promises
      but now the permanence
of disruption

this time Norma's eyes
      once radiant with love
from hope and laughter

are shining now again
      with the deeper radiance
of a joy reaped from tears

Psalm 126:5

after unspeakable loss
        the tears of unspeakable joy
    beaming toward him such brightness

from her heart's choked depths
        that all of us felt
  somehow enlightened

as children somehow refresh us
      before their eyes
  are clouded with experience

and as the book of Isaiah
        after the Temple's destruction
  and the Babylonian exile

could somehow proclaim in closing
      You will go out in joy
    and be led forth in peace   *Isaiah 55:12*

to the Second Temple
      and to its destruction
  and to the astronomical   *Genesis 22:17*

diaspora

                                29 July 2018

they are playing the Peer Gynt Suite
       the school woke up to
   when after the trauma

of failing at Oxford
       I taught young children
   My new life in a remote valley

seemed then to be circumscribed
       but in fact had been opened up –
   my brilliant prospects gone

I could be guided instead
       in moments like this one
   by whatever it is

that speaks to me now
in music

jellyfish wander like thoughts
within their closeted
simulation of an ocean
ignorant not just of roots but even

of what it is to have a floor
I watch them and for a moment sink
into that ease just before sleep
when I too become floorless

In the lobby later, I watch
the crowds pouring by
as intensely as the mackerel
in the window just above them
obsessed
with getting somewhere

A NINETY-YEAR-OLD REREADS
THE *VITA NUOVA*

To my beloved wife, Ronna Kabatznick
And in loving memory of Lu Ellen Schafer (d. 2019)

i

Rereading the *Vita Nuova*
at the age of ninety
I at last understand
why Dante who could write
like *a tailor threading his needle*   *Inferno xv.21*
phrased the *Vita* in abstractions
like *courtesy* and *beatitude*
with no colour in his lady's eyes
a symbolic *subdued crimson* for her dress   *Vita Nuova ii*

I recognize in myself
that ancient flame   *Purgatorio xxx.48;*
blinding him to the sewage   *cf. Aeneid iv.23*
in the streets of Florence
where he and his own in-laws
would soon be at war

ii

It was right after Vietnam
      you and I were so powerfully in love
   on Shattuck Avenue

that when the light in front of us
        foolishly turned red
    it was unable to stop us

we kept on laughing
        fixed on each others' eyes
    as we breezed through the night traffic

though the cars had headlights
        we did not see them
    and the closer the honking got

the more comical it was
        poor cars! poor drivers!
    what did they know?

they just couldn't understand
        you now dead and I
    were invincible

on another plane

                            iii

Should I now call this folly?
you who I first saw from afar
in your red dress
were just nineteen
when in my office hour   sensing
far better than I my inner sadness
you told me shyly you had said to Paul
you loved me

at first this left me perplexed
inspiring me to write of *Frankenstein*
how Percy's *erratic energy*
marred by abstractness and eccentricity
disrupted the lives of women around him

but you with the confidence of youth
persuaded me not to condemn our age
because of the behaviour of its monsters

and when we stood facing each other
on the islet we had swum out to
away from the rest
naked   not sexual yet
everyone in that group was naked
as was common on beaches and mountain trails

we two were drawn for a moment out of time
by that same unsolved mystery
that draws turtlets   the moment
they are freed from the shell of their egg
directly towards the ocean

I chose to be guided by you
and when on a warm January day
to the soft adagios of the pacific ocean
I drank champagne from your sweet navel
we were the *Song of Songs*

Dante was not yet thirty
when he wrote the *Vita Nuova*
empowering him to write
things never said before of any woman
which in time would soothe
embattled Florence
Europe America

But Dante   dead at fifty-six
and me   a midlife academic
not quite fifty –
he   wedded at twelve
me   halfway to an undesired divorce –
what could we then know

of this love beyond words
tranquility in old age   *Zhuangzi*
when my dear wife of three decades
in response to my unspoken prayer
and asleep

leans against me

THE FIRST TIME

To Raquelli

The first time
       it was just a gentle
   tap of a balloon

back to a three-year-old
       who chose to return it
   with another tap

till the balloon sailed back and forth
       above the table crowded
   with bottles and wine glasses

The second time
       two months later
   at a large family gathering

she came to me
       together with her mother,
   who explained *she wants to see you,*

there was no balloon
       but when she made a tent
   of her jacket over her head

I did the same
       and twenty minutes later
   she came back by herself

and at last spoke to me
to say *do it again*

The young nubile blonde
        in spotless white
    offered him a drink

sponged his face with care
        fixed a line from his index finger
    to an oxymeter on the bedside table

and having thus incapacitated him
        she then began to undo
    his difficult buckle ·

unzipped his fly
        eased down his underpants
    and leaving him uncertain

how he should respond
        she deftly manipulated
    – this being to her old hat –

his penis
into a bottle

Utterly helpless
        he was astonished
    how beautiful she was

with the bright light behind her face
        he was overwhelmed with sudden love
    not only for her

but for everyone
even her other patients

PIG

We climbed with our bikes
        onto the back of a battered pickup
   and found ourselves for an hour

eye to eye with a huge pig
        whose four feet were all safely tethered
   so we were shocked when on arriving

in a Breton village
        the pig was brutally tumbled
   into a waist-deep tub

to be slaughtered by the driver with a knife
        cutting first the tendons to its legs
   and then its throat

and when the pig stopped squealing
        he cut out its testes and held them up
   with a wild twisted grin

of victory over his foe
        At that moment his grimace seemed inhuman
   but later I had to suspect

that perhaps it was all too human
        Was it my own sheltered life
   that was unreal

cut off from the raw facts
           of a world of survival
      dependent on slaughter?

Or – I need to ask
           now I am ninety-three –
      is there more at stake in life

than this kingdom of death?

THE BALLAD OF JAKE AND JAYME

*Cf. Matt Furrer and Mitch Smith, "Days of Plotting
To Kidnap a Girl Seen by Chance," New York Times,
15 January 2019.*

From the moment Jake
        driving to his second day
    at the cheese factory

by chance for the first time
        saw Jayme
    boarding a middle-school bus

he knew *that was the girl*
        he was going to take
    His desire for her

was so great
        he switched his license plates
    bought a mask from Walmart

drove to the Closs home
        and in the space of four minutes
    shot the father and mother

whom he had never met
        then kidnapped Jayme
    from her hiding place in the bath

For eighty-eight days
        he had his way with her
    keeping her when he had guests

boxed under his bed
        with *totes and laundry bins*
   weighted down with barbells

What was it in him made him
        tell her he would be gone
   for a few hours

giving her time to escape?
        What made him a twenty-one-year-old
   balding man

tell the police
        he knew why they had stopped him
  "I did it"

He had feelings for her
        what a tragedy
   he had so few

for himself

SURPRISE

The smile and the voice that he knows to be lost
are the fundamental origin of his work.

Jorge Luis Borges, "Beatrice's Last Smile"

It was not her holy deeds that lifted Dante
To contemplate perfection. No – all it took
Was her simple beauty, a gracious smile,
And one kind word, spoken very gently,

For him to change our history with his book
Of human depravity and elevation.
We too can learn from a human face
To seek nobility in moderation.

Last night, for example, I was surprised
How a stranger's gentle discourse on the terrace
Of a penthouse, towering over tenements,
And her smile, revealing her human kindness,

Made me see again, as did Dante once,
We must make this world a fairer place.

10 June 2017

For Cassie in Winnipeg

February
        and once again
    star magnolia petals

snowing

at ninety-one
my left leg gimpy

my first day ever
out with a cane

the push of lawn grass
under foot

my shadow
on the irises

I am one of five poets in Berkeley, in a poetry group, the Quincunx, that we think has evolved away from the poetry workshops we have been in for decades. Those workshops, as their name itself suggests, connote the idea of a poem as an artifact, something wrought and then polished collectively, like the "well-wrought urn" of the 1950s New Criticism, or the product of a Renaissance artist's atelier. There is a shared ambition to be "original," to create an autonomous work that has successfully liberated itself, like a non-fungible token, from the shadows of outside influence.

The five of us, in contrast, have come more and more to see our creative activity as not independent, but instead as participating in a larger cultural process, where our work serves some larger human goal, not fully understandable by us, but certainly beyond our own personal intentions. After trying for years to "be here now," we now also try to write poems that somehow resonate with the riches of our culture's past, and also its future. In this we are conscious of our debt to two poets some of us came to know (and write about) here in Berkeley: Czeslaw Milosz and Denise Levertov.

ESPRIT DE L'ESCALIER

Belated response to friends who asked me to give,
in one sentence, the message of my forthcoming book,
Reading the Dream

This is the word of the Lord unto Zerubbabel, saying,
Not by might, nor by power, but by my spirit, saith the Lord
of hosts.

Zechariah 4:6

— why didn't I simply say

people like us here
at this Chanukah table
should not just talk about politics

which let's face it
we can do nothing about
we should talk about culture

preparing people's minds
for tomorrow's revolution
and if pain like Blake's

in the left foot forces us
to be poets who mind
we can turn to the black windshield

in front of our eyes
smeared by journalists academics
and worst of all our friends

with the grime of facts
and clean it a bit with hope
hope powerful because

it has always been there
in the minds of those most healthy
while we wait for the great poet

on whose shoulder
that eagle flying
above and ahead of us

in the darkness
will come down briefly to rest

7 December 2023

"*Shiva Candle*"

Blinova, Ekaterina. "Michael Hudson: De-Dollarization is Remedy Against US Militarism." *Sputnik International*, 9 June 2023. https://sputnikglobe. com/20230609/michael-hudson-de-dollarization-is-remedy-against-us-militarism-1111033558.html.

Liteky, Charlie. "Praise for *Renunciation*, the Story of Charlie Liteky's Pilgrimage from Catholic Military Chaplain, Vietnam Hawk, and Medal of Honor Recipient – to Civilian Warrior for Peace." Accessed 27 October 2023. http://www.charlieliteky.org/his-book-renunciation.html.

"*Bob Silvers and the Deep State*"

Djwa, Sandra. *The Politics of the Imagination: A Life of F.R. Scott.* Vancouver: Douglas & McIntyre, 1989.

Ellsberg, Daniel. "Laos: What Nixon Is Up To." *New York Review of Books*, 11 March 2019, 71. http://www.nybooks.com/articles/1971/03/11/laos-what-nixon-is-up-to.

Finley, M.I. "The Origins of Christianity." Review of Maurice Goguel, *The Primitive Church. New York Review of Books*, 20 August 1964. http://www.nybooks.com/articles/1964/08/20/the-origins-of-christianity.

Foucault, Michel. *The Archaeology of Knowledge; and, The Discourse on Language*. New York: Pantheon Books, 1972.

Grim, Ryan. "Kill The Messenger: How The Media Destroyed Gary Webb." *Huffpost*, 10 October 2014. https://www.huffingtonpost.com/2014/10/10/kill-the-messenger_n_5962708.html. (Full disclosure: I was a consultant on the screenplay of the referenced film.)

Hanyok, Robert J. "Skunks, Bogies, Silent Hounds, and the Flying Fish." Naval Historical Center, Department of the Navy. http://www.ibiblio.org/hyperwar/NHC/skunks.htm#fn106.

Harding, D.W. "Good-by Man." Review of Michel Foucault, *The Order of Things: An Archeology of the Human Sciences*. *New York Review of Books*, 12 August 1971. http://www.nybooks.com/articles/1971/08/12/good-by-man.

Hitchens, Christopher. "The Persian Version." *Atlantic*, July–August 2006. https://www.theatlantic.com/magazine/archive/2006/07/the-persian-version/304961.

Johnson, Lyndon B. *The Vantage Point: Perspectives on the Presidency, 1963–1969*. New York: Holt, Rinehart and Winston, 1971.

Judt, Tony. "The 'Problem of Evil' in Postwar Europe." *New York Review of Books*, 14 February 2008. http://www.nybooks.com/articles/2008/02/14/the-problem-of-evil-in-postwar-europe.

Kermode, Frank. "Crisis Critic." Review of Michel Foucault, *The Archaeology of Knowledge and The Discourse on Language*. *New York Review of Books*, 1973. http://www.nybooks.com/articles/1973/05/17/crisis-critic.

Kimball, Roger. "A nostalgia for Molotovs: 'The New York Review.'" *New Criterion*, April 1998. http://www.newcriterion.com/articles.cfm/A-nostalgia-for-Molotovs---ldquo-The-New-York-Review-rdquo--3067.

Kopkind, Andrew. *The Thirty Years War: Dispatches and Diversions of a Radical Journalist*. London: Verso, 1996.

Levingston, Steven. "Glenn Beck's paranoid thriller, 'The Overton Window.'" *Washington Post*, 15 June 2010. http://www.washingtonpost.com/wp-dyn/content/article/2010/06/14/AR2010061405423.html. ("Under this theory, put forward by public policy expert Joseph Overton, the public is willing to consider only a few ideas or scenarios as reasonable – those are the ones that reside within the window. Radical notions remain outside the window, unfit for serious debate.")

Lilla, Mark. "Robert B. Silvers (1929–2017)." *New York Review of Books*, 11 May 2017. http://www.nybooks.com/articles/2017/05/11/robert-silvers-tributes.

Merton, Thomas. *Raids on the Unspeakable*. New York: New Directions, 1966.

Milosz, Czeslaw. *The Captive Mind*. New York: Vintage, 1990.

– *Native Realm: A Search for Self-Definition*. Translated by Catherine S. Leach. New York: Farrar, Strauss and Giroux, 2002.

– "Treatise of Poetry." *New and Collected Poems*. New York: Ecco, 2003.

Popkin, Richard H. *The Second Oswald: A Startling Alternative to the Single Assassin Theory of the Warren Commission Report*. New York: Avon, 1966.

Proctor, Pat. *Containment and Credibility: The Ideology and Deception That Plunged America into the Vietnam War*. New York: Carrel Books, 2016.

Scott, Peter Dale. *Coming to Jakarta: A Poem About Terror*. New York: New Directions, 1989.

– "Old Wealth, the Kuomintang, and the CIA's Air America." *Asia-Pacific Journal*, 22 September 2022. https://apjjf.org/2022/16/Scott.html.

– *Poetry and Terror*. With Freeman Ng. Lanham, MD: Lexington. 2018.

– "Tonkin Bay: Was There a Conspiracy?" Review of Joseph Goulden, *Truth Is the First Casualty*. *New York Review of Books*, 29 January 1970, 31–41.

– *The War Conspiracy: JFK, 9/11, and the Deep Politics of War*. New York: Skyhorse, 2013.

Shattuck, Roger. "The Reddening of America." Review of V.S. Naipaul, *A Turn in the South*. *New York Review of Books*, 30 March 1989. http://www.nybooks.com/articles/1989/03/30/the-reddening-of-america.

Sherman, Scott. "The Rebirth of the NYRB." *The Nation*, 20 May 2004, 5. https://www.thenation.com/article/rebirth-nyrb. (Quoting Stanley Hoffmann.)

Stroud, Matt, "The Unbelievable Life and Death of Michael C. Ruppert." *The Verge*, 22 July 2014. https://www.theverge.com/2014/7/22/5881501/the-unbelievable-life-and-death-of-michael-c-ruppert.

Tracy, James F. "The CIA and the Media: 50 Facts the World Needs to Know." *InfoWars*, 5 September 2015. https://www.infowars.com/the-cia-and-the-media-50-facts-the-world-needs-to-know (defunct link).

Whitney, Joel. *Finks: How the CIA Tricked the World's Best Writers*. New York: OR Books, 2016.

Woods, Randall Bennett. *Fulbright: A Biography*. Cambridge: Cambridge University Press, 1995.

Scott, Peter Dale. "Vital Artifice: Mary, Percy, and the Psychological Integrity of *Frankenstein.*" In *The Endurance of Frankenstein: Essays on Mary Shelley's Novel,* edited by George Levine and U.C. Knoepflmacher, 188, 191, 185 (Berkeley: University of California Press, 1979).

"Dreamcraft"

Clarkson, Adrienne. *Norman Bethune.* Toronto: Penguin Canada, 2011. 112.

Dostoyevsky, Fyodor. *Crime and Punishment.* London: Collier, 1917. 424. ("I wanted to have the daring.")

Ferrone, Vincenzo. *The Enlightenment: History of an Idea.* Translated by Elisabetta Tarantino. Princeton: Princeton University Press, 2015. 46–7.

Goethe, Johann Wolfgang von. *Dichtung und Wahrheit.* Edited by Parke Godwin. London: Wiley and Putnam, 1847. 42, 49.

Gordon, Lyndall. *T.S. Eliot: An Imperfect Life.* New York: Norton, 1998. 511, citing letter of 2 June 1950.

Graham, Ron. "Paterson Ewen: The Artist's Dilemma." *Canadian Art* (Fall 1996): 70–9. http://canadianart.ca/features/1996/09/01/paterson-ewen-the-artists-dilemma.

Heidegger, Martin. *Kant and the Problem of Metaphysics.* Translated by Richard Taft. Bloomington: Indiana University Press, 1990. 286.

Jordan, Jonathan W. *American Warlords: How Roosevelt's High Command Led America to Victory in World War II.* New York: NAL Caliber, 2015. 331–2.

Lowe, Peter. "Prufrock in St Petersburg: The Presence of Dostoyevsky's Crime and Punishment in T.S. Eliot's 'The Love Song of J. Alfred Prufrock'." *Journal of Modern Literature* (2005): 1–24.

Marshall, Tom. *Multiple Exposures, Promised Lands: Essays on Canadian Poetry and Fiction.* Kingston: Quarry Press, 1992. 57.

May, Robert G. "F.R. Scott, the FLQ, and the October Crisis." *Quebec Studies* (22 March 2013). https://www.highbeam.com/doc/1G1-346808478.html.

Mickiewicz, Adam. "The Romantic." Translated by W.H. Auden. In Czeslaw Milosz, *The Land of Ulro*, translated by Louis Iribarne (New York: Farrar, Straus and Giroux, 1984), 99.

Milosz, Czeslaw. "Treatise on Theology." Translated by Robert Hass. In *Second Space: New Poems*, 51 (New York: Ecco, 2004).

– *The Witness of Poetry*. Cambridge, MA: Harvard University Press, 1983. 41–2.

Sachar, Howard M. *The Assassination of Europe, 1918–1942: A Political History.* Toronto: University of Toronto Press, 2015. ("Dollfuss's spacious office was luxuriously furnished with eighteenth-century furniture, artifacts, and paintings. The adjoining 'Hall of Mirrors,' equally sumptuous, was used for cabinet meetings ... [By 12:55 p.m. on 25 July 1934], the seat of Austrian government was in the control of 154 Nazi putschists ... Yet before Dollfuss could react, his personal attendant, Eduard Hedvicek, suddenly pulled the chancellor by the arm, urging him ... to come with him. They could escape the building altogether, Hedvicek explained, through a side exit ... Dollfuss complied. But to both men's consternation, they found the exit door locked" [210].)

Scott, Peter Dale. *Minding the Darkness: A Poem for the Year 2000*. New York: New Directions, 2000. 6.

Enlightenment

Nyctinasty n. "a nastic movement (as the opening and closing of some flowers) that is associated with diurnal changes of temperature or light intensity" (Merriam Webster). Sometimes distinguished from photonasty and thermonasty.

Hu, Can-Ming Hu. *Interplay of Spins: Charges and Photons in Low-Dimensional Systems*. Göttingen: Cuvillier Verlag, 2005. ("The microscopic high-frequency field which an electron feels contains always two parts: the external one and the one from its surrounding, the later [*sic*] is related to the change of the electron-electron interaction induced by the external field" [104].)

Swanson, John. *God, Science and the Universe: The Integration of Religion and Science*. New York: Eloquent Books, 2010. 79.

"To Czeslaw Milosz"

"Álvar Núñez Cabeza de Vaca." *Wikipedia*. Last edited 14 October 2023. https://en.wikipedia.org/wiki/%C3%81lvar_N%C3%BA%C3%B1ez_Cabeza_de_Vaca.

Cohen, Robert. *Freedom's Orator: Mario Savio and the Radical Legacy of the 1960s*. Oxford: Oxford University Press, 2009.

Merton, Thomas, and Czeslaw Milosz. *Striving Towards Being: The Letters of Thomas Merton and Czeslaw*

Milosz. Edited by Robert Faggan. New York: Farrar, Strauss and Giroux, 1997.

Milosz, Czeslaw. *Milosz's ABCs*. Farrar, Strauss and Giroux, 2002. [*ABCs*]

– *Native Realm: A Search for Self-Definition*. Translated by Catherine S. Leach. New York: Farrar, Strauss and Giroux, 2002.

– *New and Collected Poems*. New York: Ecco, 2003. [*NCP*]

– ed. *Postwar Polish Poetry*. Oakland: University of California Press, 1983.

– *Second Space: New Poems*. Reprint. New York: Ecco, 2004.

– *A Treatise on Poetry*. Translated by Czeslaw Milosz and Robert Hass. New York: Ecco, 2001.

"The Forest of Wishing"

Epigraph appears in Czeslaw Milosz, "Throughout Our Lands," *New and Collected Poetry* (New York: Ecco, 2003), 188.

This poem was written in perhaps 1962, shortly after my arrival in California from my Canadian government job in Warsaw. The Bay Area at the time was still in the innocent stages of an erotic revolution; the Robespierres had not yet inflicted on the young the cruel deceits of the Sexual Freedom League and "The Summer of Love."

My colleague Tom Parkinson held a large party at his home for one of the minor San Francisco Beat Poets. As a Canadian I was quite unprepared for a long eroticized conversation I had there with a striking blonde of about twenty; still less when at the end of it she made me promise to call about seeing her again in her San Francisco apartment.

Shortly afterwards I wrote this poem, which poured out all at once, not bothering to explain itself. And as I was only six years into a young and happy marriage with two small children, I thought back and forth before finally making a phone call. To my relief, she no longer remembered anything about me or the promise.

About this time I had translated with Czeslaw Milosz his polysemous poem "Throughout Our Lands" (*Encounter*, February 1964, 46–9). Like myself, Milosz was newly arrived from Europe, with a reaction to California unlike anything in his other translated poems, and less Canadian than mine:

Who has not dreamt of the Marquis de Sade's chateaux?
When one ("ah-h-h!") rubs his hands
and to the job: to gouge with a spur
young girls drawn up in line for a footrace
or to order naked nuns in black net stockings
to lash us with a whip as we bite the bedsheets.

In the poem's last section Milosz speaks in the voice of the sixteenth-century voyager Cabeza de Vaca, who survived the shipwreck of his European ship to find himself among

The hu-hu-hu of tribes, hot bramble of the continent.
But afterward? Who am I, the lace of cuffs
Not mine, the table carved with lions not mine,
    Dona Clara's
Fan, the slipper from under her gown – hell, no.
On all fours! On all fours!
Smear our thighs with war paint.
Lick the ground. Wha wha, hu hu.

As Milosz later explained in prose: "After everything he'd seen, all the products of civilization seemed artificial." Which, after all, they are.

"A Ninety-Year-Old Rereads *the* Vita Nuova"

Scott, Peter Dale. "Vital Artifice: Mary, Percy, and the Psychological Integrity of *Frankenstein*." In *The Endurance of Frankenstein: Essays on Mary Shelley's Novel*, edited by George Levine and U.C. Knoepflmacher, 172–3 (Berkeley: University of California Press, 1979).

ACKNOWLEDGMENTS

Several poems previously appeared in the following publications:

"Presence," "Moreness," "Deep Movements," "Mythogenesis," and "Esprit de l'escalier" as "Appendix" in Peter Dale Scott, *Reading the Dream: A Post-Secular History of Enmindment* (Lanham, MD: Rowman & Littlefield, 2024).

"Shiva Candle": *American Exception, "Shiva Candle – A Poem for Daniel Ellsberg,"* 16 August 2023, YouTube video, 3:52, https://youtu.be/Vvct59eYOiQ.

"Leonard and Peter": Leonard Cohen, *The Flame*, edited by Robert Faggen (New York: Farrar, Straus, Giroux, 2018), 159–60.

"The Condition of Water": *Rattle*, December 2018, https://www.rattle.com/the-condition-of-water-by-peter-dale-scott.

"The Forest of Wishing": *Times Literary Supplement* (London) 3,316 (16 September 1965): 798.

"To Czeslaw Milosz": Peter Dale Scott, *Ecstatic Pessimist: Czeslaw Milosz, Poet of Catastrophe and Hope* (Lanham, MD: Rowman & Littlefield, 2023), 258–63.

"After Sixty-Four Years": *Dhamma Moon*, 22 December 2017, http://dhammamoon.org/poems/peter-dale-scott/after-64-years.

I also want to acknowledge the vital help I received in editing this book from my daughter, Cassie Scott, and her wife, Helene Vosters.